OTIS REDDING
GREATEST HITS

PIANO
VOCAL
GUITAR

CHICAGO PUBLIC LIBRARY

R02080 23486

D1452178

All photos courtesy of Zelma Atwood Redding

ISBN 0-634-03206-2

HAL•LEONARD®
CORPORATION

7777 W. BLUEMOUND RD. P.O. BOX 13819 MILWAUKEE, WI 53213

For all works contained herein:
Unauthorized copying, arranging, adapting, recording or public performance is an infringement of copyright.
Infringers are liable under the law.

Visit Hal Leonard Online at
www.halleonard.com

CHICAGO PUBLIC LIBRARY
WEST ENGLEWOOD BRANCH
1745 W. 63rd STREET
CHICAGO, IL 60636

R02080 23486

CONTENTS

OTIS REDDING
(1941—1967)

Otis Redding was born on September 9, 1941, in Dawson, Georgia, the son of a Baptist minister. When he was five his family moved to Macon, Georgia, and at an early age he began his career as a singer and musician in the choir of the Vineville Baptist Church. Otis attended Ballad Hudson High School and participated in the school band. Determined to help his family financially, he dropped out of high school and went on to work with Little Richard's former band, the Upsetters. He also began to compete in local talent shows for the top prize of five dollars. After winning fifteen times straight, he was no longer allowed to compete.

In 1959, Otis sang at the Grand Duke Club. He joined Johnny Jenkins and The Pinetoppers in 1960 and also sang in the "Teenage Party" talent shows sponsored by the King Bee, Hamp Swain, a local celebrity disc jockey. Held initially at the Roxy Theater, these talent shows were later moved to the Douglass Theater in Macon.

In October, 1962 Johnny Jenkins and The Pinetoppers drove to Memphis, Tennessee for a recording session at Stax Records. The session didn't go well, so Stax co-owner Jim Stewart allowed Otis to cut a couple of songs with the studio time that had been booked. The result was "These Arms of Mine," released that same year. This was the first of many hit singles, including "I've Been Loving You Too Long," "Respect," and "Try a Little Tenderness." Nine months later he was invited to perform at the Apollo Theater for a live recording. That performance included "Shake" and "Satisfaction" and the sold-out audience refused to let him go until he came back onstage for an encore.

As a performer Otis Redding appeared throughout the United States, Canada, Europe and the Caribbean. His concert tours were among the biggest box office successes of any touring performer at that time. In 1967 he was nominated in three categories by the National Academy of Recording Arts and Sciences, but 1968 was destined to be a banner year, with appearances in New York's Philharmonic Hall and Washington's Constitution Hall. Additionally, Otis was booked for several major television network appearances, including *The Ed Sullivan Show* and *The Smothers Brothers Show*. He even starred in a television special.

In 1970 Warner Brothers released an album of live recordings from the 1967 Monterey International Pop Festival; it featured Otis Redding on one side and Jimi Hendrix on the other. The record is evidence that hip white audiences, better known as the "love crowd," appreciated Otis Redding just as much as the black audiences for whom he had always played. His energy and excitement, his showmanship, and his relationship with the crowd made Redding a master performer capable of reaching audiences the world over.

Although much has been made of his gifts as a performer, it was his music, composed and arranged by Otis himself, that lead to his commercial success. Three of his compositions alone accounted for over three and one half million record sales. Unquestionably his biggest hit was "(Sittin' On) The Dock of the Bay." Unlike anything he had ever written, it was influenced by his admiration for the Beatles' classic *Sgt. Pepper's Lonely Hearts Club Band*. Otis had played their album constantly during a week he spent on a houseboat in Sausalito, while performing at San Francisco's Fillmore West Theater in the summer of 1967. It was there, inspired by the stunning location, that he composed what would become his signature tune.

In 1965 Otis formed his own record label, Jotis Records, but he was also active in other business ventures within his native state, including real estate, investments, stocks and bonds. He was even president of his own publishing company, Redwal Music Co., Inc., and was active in its operation. To date, the company has copyrighted over 200 commercially successful songs, many of which have sold in excess of one million copies.

Beyond his success in the music industry, Otis was a family man. He met Zelma Atwood in 1959, and they were married in August of 1961. Together they have four children: Dexter, Karla, Otis III and Demetria, who was adopted after his death. In 1965 he moved them into a spacious 300 acre property, located in Round Oak, Georgia, just outside of Macon. "The Big O Ranch," affectionately named after "The Big O" himself, included a two story brick home, plenty of livestock and a 3.5 acre lake.

Today sons Dexter and Otis III are active as music producers and songwriters. Karla is a successful and influential entrepreneur. She founded Karla's Shoe Boutique, which she manages with the help of her mother and partner in

downtown Macon. Demetria is a radio producer at WIBB, radio 97.9, also in Macon. Zelma, executress of the Redding Estate, manages the daily requests for song usage in commercials, music sampling, use of name and likeness, and the Scholarship Foundation.

Over the years Otis Redding has received numerous awards and honors. In 1966 *Melody Maker Magazine* of London, England awarded him International Male Vocalist of the Year. (Elvis Presley had "owned" this award for ten years prior to Redding's selection.) In 1989 he was inducted into the Rock and Roll Hall of Fame; in 1993 the United States Postal Service issued a stamp; in 1994 the National Academy of Popular Music presented Otis with a Songwriters Hall of Fame induction. Most recently, in 1999, Redding was given a Lifetime Achievement Grammy by the National Academy of Recording Arts and Sciences

On December 10, 1967, while flying his twin-engine Beechcraft near Madison, Wisconsin, Otis Redding crashed into Lake Monona. Though cut down in his prime, Otis, the man *and* his music, continues to impact the world.

AMEN

By OTIS REDDING

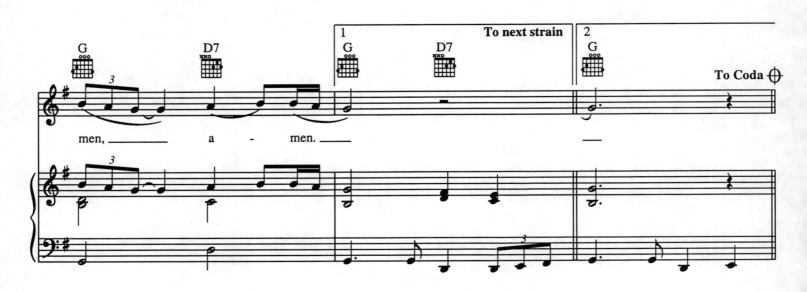

Copyright © 1968 IRVING MUSIC, INC.
Copyright Renewed
All Rights Reserved   Used by Permission

8

shine, ___ to show my love. ___ 2. One thing my pap-py used to say. He say that

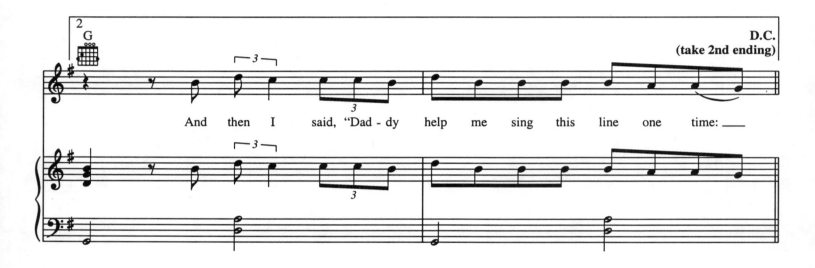

And then I said, "Dad - dy help me sing this line one time: ___

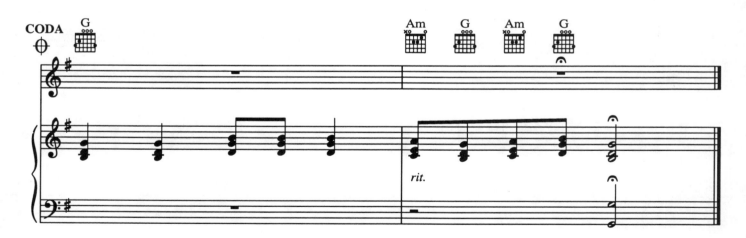

rit.

Additional Lyrics

2. One thing my pappy used to say. He say that
"Even in my home, son, (I said, 'What, dad?')
I'm gonna let it shine. (He said:)
Even in your home, son,
You've got to let your little light shine.

Even in your home, son,
You've got to let it shine.
Just let it shine, just let it shine,
To show your love."
And then I said, "Daddy, help me sing this line one time."
To Chorus

CHAINED AND BOUND

Words and Music by
OTIS REDDING

Slowly

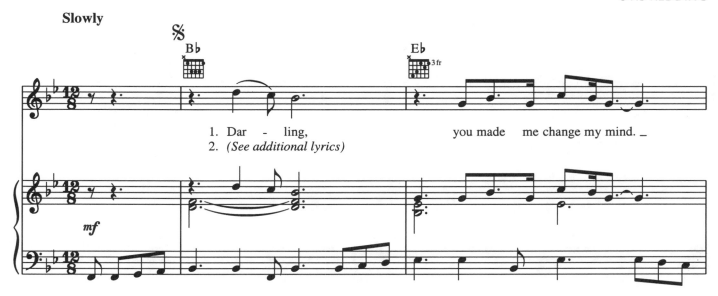

1. Dar - ling, you made me change my mind. _
2. *(See additional lyrics)*

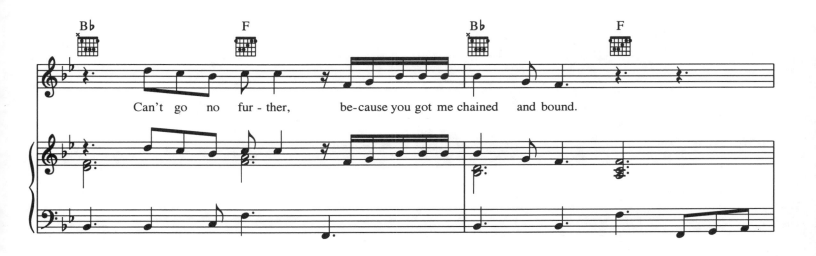

Can't go no fur - ther, be-cause you got me chained and bound.

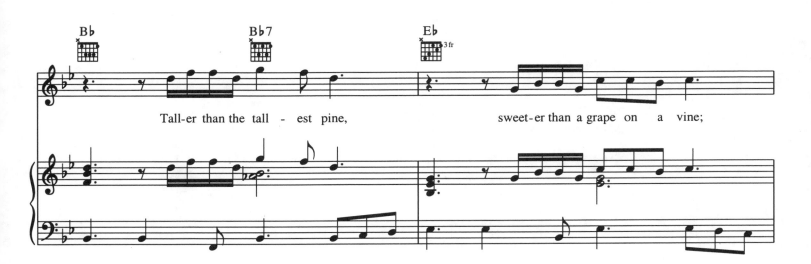

Tall-er than the tall - est pine, sweet-er than a grape on a vine;

Copyright © 1964 IRVING MUSIC, INC.
Copyright Renewed
All Rights Reserved   Used by Permission

give me? __   Feel   like stand-ing up and tell-ing the world   I'm chained to your love.

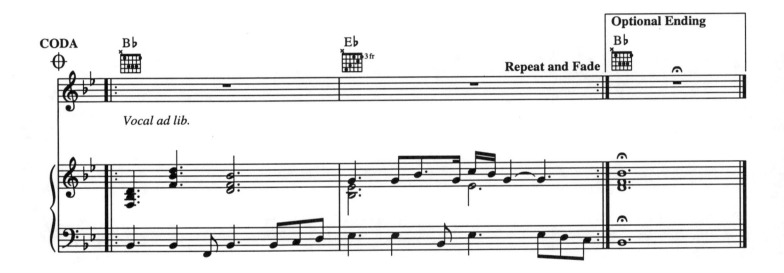

Vocal ad lib.

Additional Lyrics

2. Darling, don't break this little heart of mine.
   There's no greater love than the love of yours and mine.
   Walk with your head in the sky; darling, don't ever pass me by.
   I ain't goin' no further, 'cause you got me chained and bound.

FA-FA-FA-FA-FA
(Sad Song)

Words and Music by OTIS REDDING
and STEVE CROPPER

Copyright © 1966 IRVING MUSIC, INC.
Copyright Renewed
All Rights Reserved   Used by Permission

14

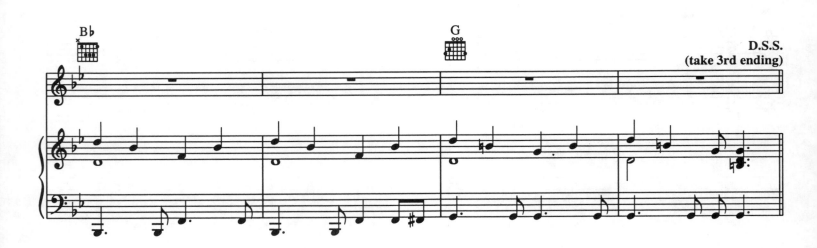

Additional Lyrics

All my life I been singing sad songs,
Trying to get my message to you, honey.
But this the only song, y'all, I can sing,
And when I get to singing, my message be to you. It goes:
To Chorus

HARD TO HANDLE

Words and Music by ALLEN JONES,
ALVERTIS BELL and OTIS REDDING

Moderate Funk

N.C.

Bb7

1.,3. Ba - by, here I am ___ I'm a man on the scene. ___
2. (See additional lyrics)

I can give you what you want, _ but you got to go home _ with me.

I've got some good _ old lov - in' and I've got some in store. _

Copyright © 1968 IRVING MUSIC, INC.
Copyright Renewed
All Rights Reserved   Used by Permission

Additional Lyrics

2. Action speaks louder than words, and I'm a man with a great experience.
I know you got you another man, but I can love you better than him.
Take my hand, don't be afraid, I want to prove every word that I said.
I'm advertising love for free, so won't you place your ad with me?
Boys will come a dime by the dozen, but that ain't nothin' but kiss and look.
Pretty little thing, let me light the candle, 'cause mama, I'm sure hard to handle, now.

THE HAPPY SONG

Words and Music by OTIS REDDING
and STEVE CROPPER

Copyright © 1968 IRVING MUSIC, INC.
Copyright Renewed
All Rights Reserved   Used by Permission

Additional Lyrics

2. On a cold, windy, rainy night,
   She shut all my doors, she cut off the light.
   She hold me and squeeze me tight,
   She tell me: "Big O, everything's all right," and I go
   To Chorus

3. Bring my breakfast to the table;
   When I go to work she know I'm able.
   Do my job, when I come back in,
   You oughta' see my baby's face, she just grin, grin, grin.
   To Chorus

I'VE BEEN LOVING YOU TOO LONG

Words and Music by OTIS REDDING
and JERRY BUTLER

1. I've been lov-ing you _____
2.(See additional lyrics)

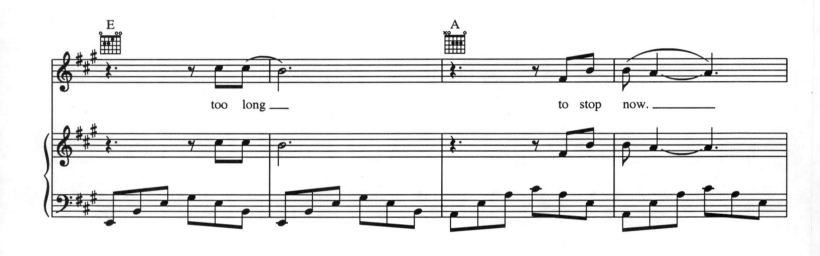

too long _____ to stop now. _____

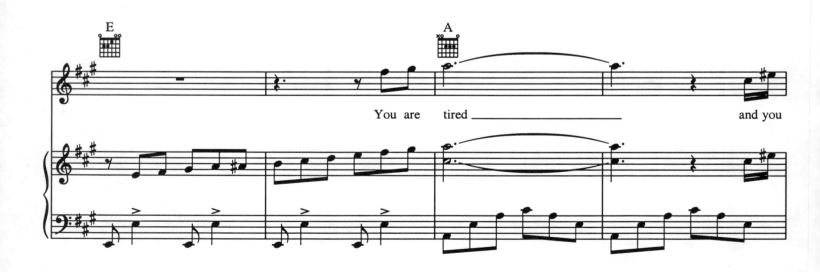

You are tired _____ and you

Copyright © 1965 IRVING MUSIC, INC.
Copyright Renewed
All Rights Reserved   Used by Permission

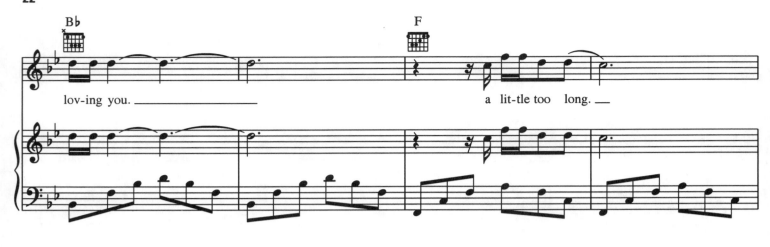

Bb

lov-ing you. _____

F

a lit-tle too long. __

Bb

I don't wan-na stop now. _____

Gb

Oh,

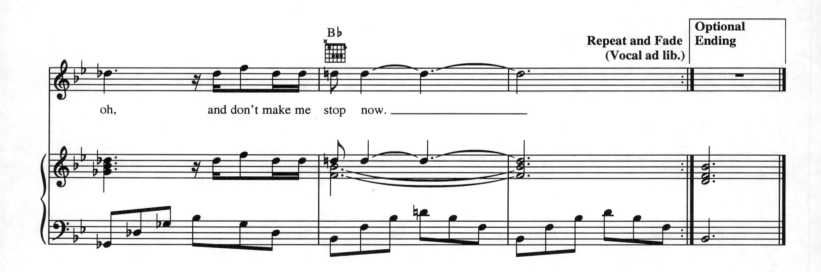

Bb

Repeat and Fade
(Vocal ad lib.)

Optional
Ending

oh,   and don't make me stop now. _____

Additional Lyrics

2. With you, my life has been so wonderful;
   I can't stop now.
   You are tired,
   And your love is growing cold;
   My love is growing stronger,
   As our affair grows old.
   I've been loving you, a little too long;
   I don't wanna stop now.

KNOCK ON WOOD

Words and Music by EDDIE FLOYD
and STEVE CROPPER

Copyright © 1966 IRVING MUSIC, INC.
Copyright Renewed
All Rights Reserved Used by Permission

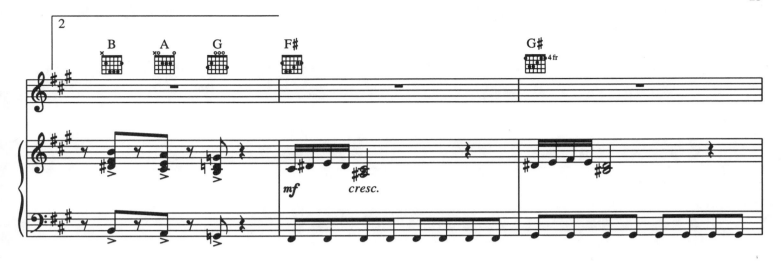

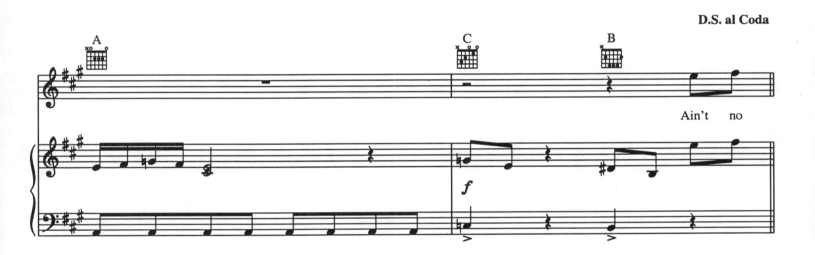

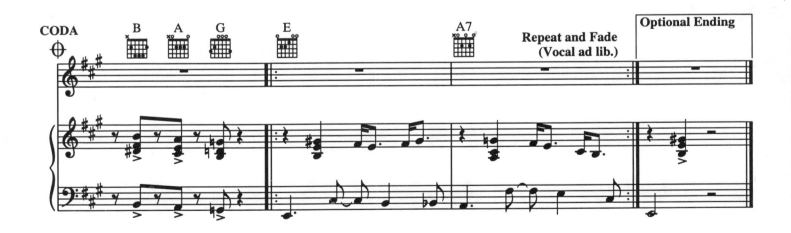

Additional Lyrics

3. Ain't no secret that a woman can feel my love come up.
   You got me seeing, she really sees that, that I get enough.
   Just one touch from you, baby, you know it means so much.
   It's like thunder, lightning;
   The way you love me is frightening,
   I think I better knock-knock-knock-knock on wood.

I'VE GOT DREAMS TO REMEMBER

Words and Music by OTIS REDDING,
ZELMA REDDING and JOE ROCK

Slowly

I've got dreams,

dreams _____ to re-mem-ber. _____   I've got dreams,

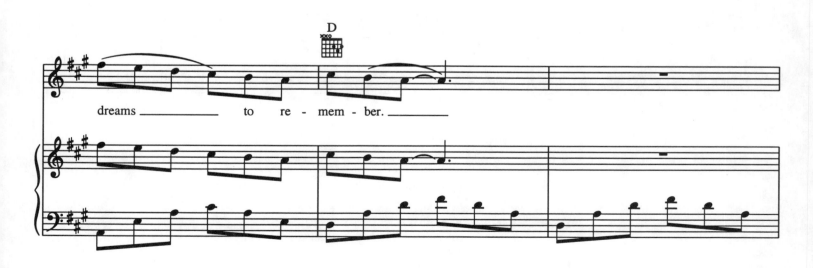

dreams _____ to re-mem-ber. _____

Copyright © 1968 IRVING MUSIC, INC.
Copyright Renewed
All Rights Reserved   Used by Permission

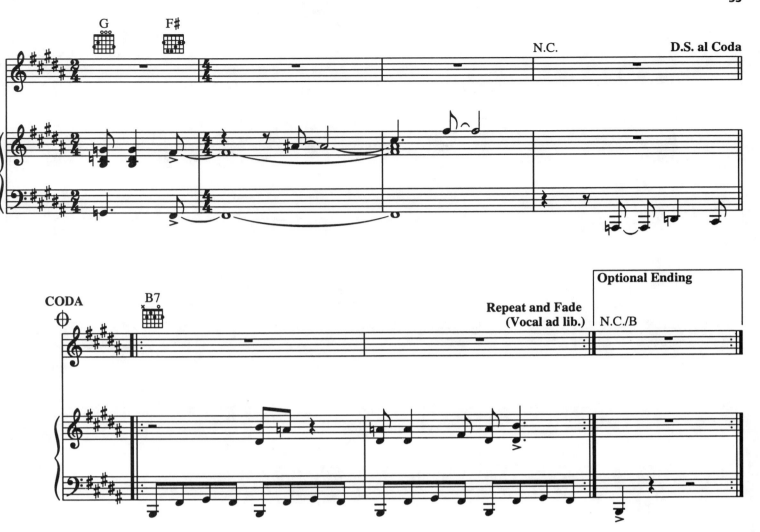

Additional Lyrics

2. Love man, that's all I am now; I'm just a
Love man, ooh baby, call me a
Love man; yes I am, I'm just a
Love man.
Which one of you girls wants me to hold you?
Which one of you girls wants me to kiss you?
Which one of you girls wants me to take you out?
I'm a love man;
I'm a love man.
To Coda

MR. PITIFUL

Words and Music by OTIS REDDING
and STEVE CROPPER

Copyright © 1965 IRVING MUSIC, INC.
Copyright Renewed
All Rights Reserved   Used by Permission

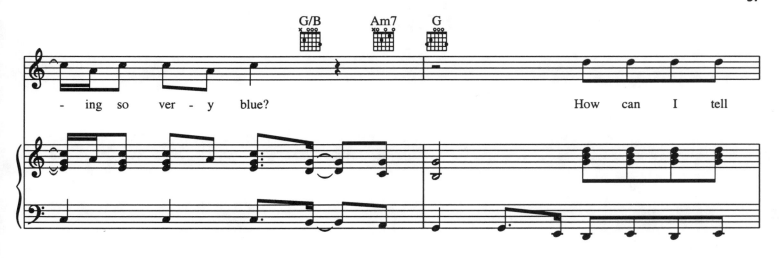

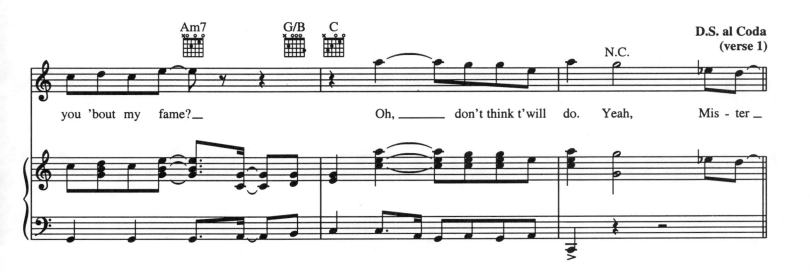

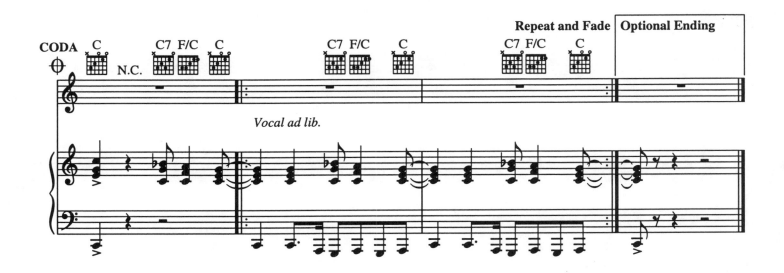

Additional Lyrics

2. They call me Mr. Pitiful; yes, everybody knows, now.
They call me Mr. Pitiful most every place I go.
But nobody seems to understand, now, what makes a man sing such a sad song,
When he lost everything, when he lost everything he had.

MY LOVER'S PRAYER

Words and Music by
OTIS REDDING

Copyright © 1966 IRVING MUSIC, INC.
Copyright Renewed
All Rights Reserved   Used by Permission

Additional Lyrics

2. My life is such a weary thing,
   But in my ears old prayers just ring and ring.
   You keep me wanting, waiting, and wishing,
   When I know deep down I'm not to blame.

3. What are you going to do tonight,
   When you need some loving arms to hold you tight?
   What are you going to do tonight,
   When you need my loving voice to tell you good night?

4. You can't let that be no problem;
   You got to come on home and help me solve all.
   Dear, I won't be missing you,
   And honey, my love affair would be all over.

5. What can the matter be?
   It can't be too serious.
   We can't talk it over, living in this misery.
   Darling, you can't make my life all over.
   Repeat Verse 4

PAIN IN MY HEART

Words and Music by
NAOMI NEVILLE

Moderate Blues Ballad

Pain in my heart, it's treat-in' me cold.

Where can my ba-by be?___ Lord,___ no one___ know.___

Pain in my heart,_____ just won't let me sleep.___

Copyright © 1964 (Renewed) by Arc Music Corporation (BMI)
International Copyright Secured   All Rights Reserved
Used By Permission

PAPA'S GOT A BRAND NEW BAG

Words and Music by
JAMES BROWN

Copyright © 1965 by Dynatone Publishing Co.
Copyright Renewed
All Rights Administered by Unichappell Music Inc.
International Copyright Secured   All Rights Reserved

RESPECT

Words and Music by
OTIS REDDING

Copyright © 1965 IRVING MUSIC, INC.
Copyright Renewed
All Rights Reserved Used by Permission

(SITTIN' ON) THE DOCK OF THE BAY

Words and Music by STEVE CROPPER
and OTIS REDDING

Copyright © 1968, 1975 IRVING MUSIC, INC.
Copyright Renewed
All Rights Reserved   Used by Permission

watch 'em roll a - way a - gain. _____ Yeah, _____ I'm
noth - in's gon - na come my _____ way. _____ So _____ I'm just gon'
make this dock my _____ home. _____ Now _____ I'm just gon'

sit - tin' on the dock of the bay, _____ watch - in' the tide _____
sit on the dock of the bay, _____
sit at the dock of the bay, _____

_____ roll _____ a - way. _____ Ooh, _____ I'm just sit - tin' on the dock of the bay,

_____ wast - in' time. _____ I

THESE ARMS OF MINE

Words and Music by
OTIS REDDING

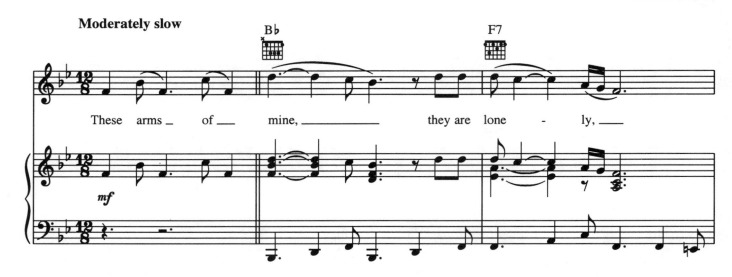

These arms _ of _ mine, _____ they are lone - ly, _

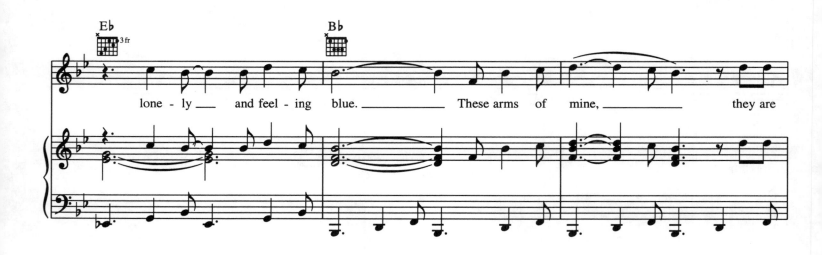

lone - ly _ and feel - ing blue. _____ These arms of mine, _____ they are

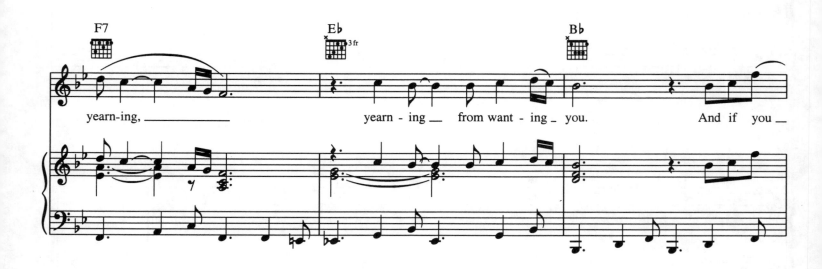

yearn-ing, _____ yearn - ing _ from want - ing _ you. And if you

Copyright © 1962 IRVING MUSIC, INC. and REGENT MUSIC CORPORATION
Copyright Renewed
All Rights Reserved   Used by Permission

56

Additional Lyrics

Come home, baby,
Just be my little woman,
Just be my lovin'
Oh, I need somebody
Oh, to treat me right,
Oh, I need two warm lovin' arms to hold me tight.
And I need your tender lips to hold me,
Oh, hold me tight.

TRAMP

Words and Music by LOWELL FULSOM
and JIMMY McCRACKLIN

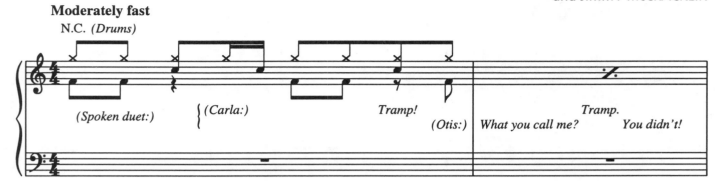

Copyright © 1966 by Careers-BMG Music Publishing, Inc. and Budget Music (BMI)/Administered by Bug Music
Copyright Renewed
International Copyright Secured   All Rights Reserved

(Otis:) Tramp?   *(Carla:)* That's right, that's what you are.

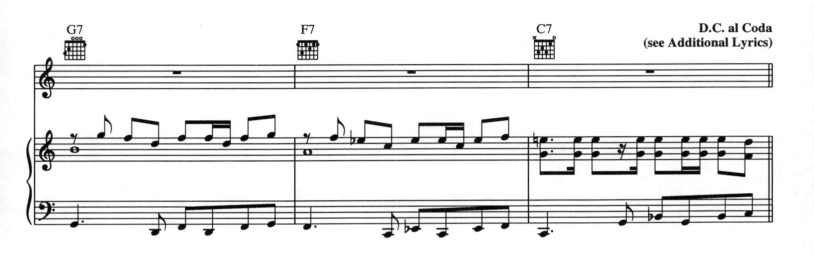

D.C. al Coda
(see Additional Lyrics)

Repeat and Fade
(Ad lib. dialogue)

Optional Ending

Additional Lyrics

Carla: You know what, Otis, I don't care what you say,
You're still a tramp.

That's right, you don't even have a fat bankroll
in your pocket. You probably haven't even got
twenty-five cents.

Otis: What?

I got six Cadillacs, five Lincolns, four Olds,
six Mercurys, three T-Birds, a Mustang...
To Chorus:

TRY A LITTLE TENDERNESS

Words and Music by HARRY WOODS,
JIMMY CAMPBELL and REG CONNELLY

Lyrics:
Oh, she may be wea-ry, and young girls, they do get wea-ry; wear-ing the same ___ shab-by dress. But

© 1932 (Renewed 1960) CAMPBELL, CONNELLY & CO., LTD.
All Rights in the United States and Canada Administered by EMI ROBBINS CATALOG INC. (Publishing) and WARNER BROS. PUBLICATIONS U.S. INC. (Print)
All Rights Reserved   Used by Permission

CODA

ten - der - ness. _____

(Vocal ad lib.)

Optional Ending

Repeat and Fade